VIA FOLIOS 88

LOVE LINES

Poems by Emanuel di Pasquale

LOVE LINES

Poems by Emanuel di Pasquale

BORDIGHERA PRESS

Library of Congress Control Number: 2013942431

© 2013 by Emanuel diPasquale

All rights reserved. Parts of this book may be reprinted only by written permission from the author, and may not be reproduced for publication in book, magazine, or electronic media of any kind, except for purposes of literary reviews by critics.

Printed in the United States.

Published by
BORDIGHERA PRESS
John D. Calandra Italian American Institute
25 West 43rd Street, 17th Floor
New York, NY 10036

VIA FOLIOS 88
ISBN 978-1-59954-053-5

For Patricia

Praise for di Pasquale's work:

"*Harvest* is a splendid collection, fresh and various."
—X. J. Kennedy

"[Di Pasquale] writes out of strong experience, and by insisting on accuracy, he comes out both simple and surprising. He's never decorative: there is always something human happening, and his words are close to it."
—Richard Wilbur

"Emanuel di Pasquale's poems should be read by every American ... He excels at the short lyric, writes directly, and feels deeply ... The reader is enriched by both his Sicilian and his American realizations in his life-enhancing lines."
—Richard Eberhart

"Emanuel di Pasquale has the ability to create what the reader needs to feel and wants to know. He lifts us with an ecstatic imagination, placing us exactly there, happily at the center, as if we've found the right dream."
—Grace Cavalieri

"Two thousand years ago a Sicilian immigrant poet named Theocritus invented the pastoral—a mode of lyrical poetry in which a sophisticated, urban imagination recaptures the pastoral in American terms in the finely observed and delicate lyrics that make up *The Silver Lake Poems*. At once innocent and sophisticated, urban and pastoral, Emanuel di Pasquale creates poetry that is timeless and direct."
—Dana Gioia

"*Escapes the Night* is even better than *Silver Lake*. It's a beautifully unfolding sequence of love poems, full of loving passages, and I think the dialogue between HE and SHE very effective. It gets a great emotion power going. Really fine. I admire the hell out of it.
—X. J. Kennedy

"Emanuel di Pasquale has composed twenty-seven musically sensual poems (*The Silver Lake Poems*). Through a woman's feelings and the suggestion of concrete imagery, he becomes a she. When 'she' gives 'him' a family ring, 'she' asks 'him' to … 'promise to dislodge / it while you fondle others'."
—Grace Cavalieri

Published poems in this collection:

"Heaven"
    THE ASBURY PARK PRESS

"Hawks at Pre-Dawn in New Jersey"
    THE ASBURY PARK PRESS

Table of Contents

Love Lines (1)
The Secret of the Narthex Stem (2)
Love Poem for Faye Dunaway (3)
Below Zero Plus (4)
Love Song for T. S. (5)
Word Song (6)
From the Daughter of Jesus (7)
Equality (9)
Early Fall East Brunswick's Pond by the Public Library (10)
Song (12)
The Dead Speak (13)
Heaven (14)
Hawks at Pre-Dawn in New Jersey (15)
To a Would-Be Iago (16)
Ragusa, Sicily (17)
A Cannon Fired a Shot (18)
Chimney Birds (19)
A Woman Runs Out of a Mental Health Clinic (20)
An End (21)
Ancestral Chimera (22)
To a Schizophrenic (23)
Faith (24)
Only (26)
From the Mountain (27)
Where are the Tamers of Horses (31)
The Dead Rise (32)
Kryseis (33)
What is the Wind (34)
Genesis (35)

Stay the Course (36)
I Sing (37)
Schizoid Carousel (38)
In the Manner of W. Shakespeare (39)
The Immortality of Nothingness (40)

ABOUT THE AUTHOR (43)

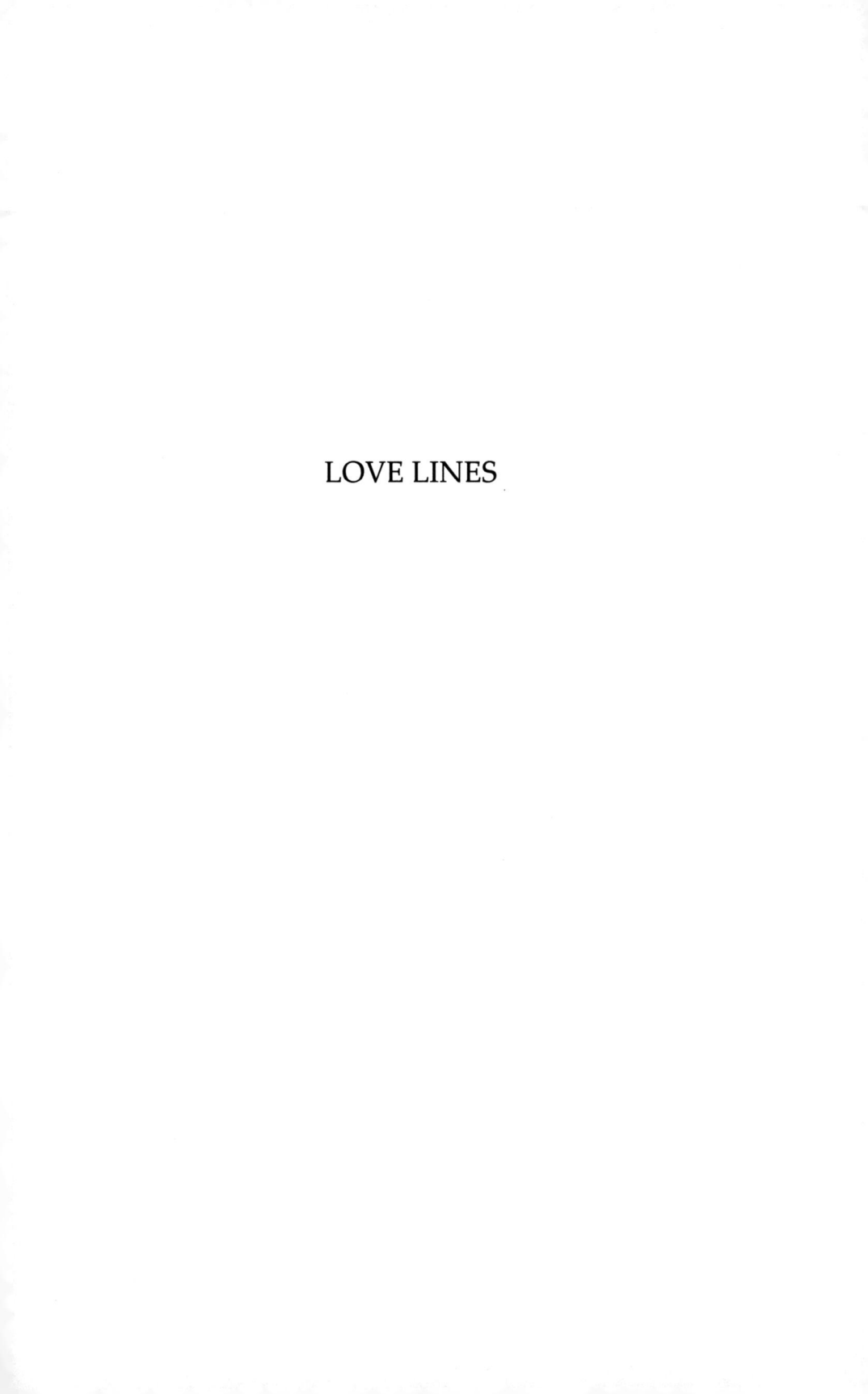

LOVE LINES

LOVE LINES

Your flesh in my hands is the root of the sunflower,
                                                   Wine

The silences of a kiss,
            Wide eyes

The supple muscles along your spine
                        Nerves alive

The Secret of the Narthex Stem

Forethought, fire,

The flower that eats air,

The fair breath of oxygen,

The secret spring

That filled the narthex stem,

That filled man and woman

With light.

Love Poem for Faye Dunaway

A fish flying over Iowa's cornfield

An airplane easing over the Mediterranean sea

A coyote howling from the moon

I am in love inside her white see-through dress

Channeling Faye's teeth

That large mouth

Such small feet

For a long-thighed woman.

Below Zero Plus

In a Golgotha-cold morning

Under a blind January sun

The sea gulls, trapeze artists,

Fly wide,

In love with freeze, light, and

                                        Spilled

Garbage

Love Song for T.S.

Could God ever create one who
Would not fall in love with you
Because of your smile?
Your Marilyn Monroe hair, sweet
Curls of grain, your
Chin falling lightly,
Your cheeks like halves
Of peach, and your eyes:
Tentative yet fully open,
Giving, and your voice,
A sweet sing song.
There is no new morning
When I looking at your
Eyes, Austrian lakes,
North Atlantic jade,
Do not fall in love
With you, ever again,
And anew.

WORD SONG

Word song be my prayer
Be prayer
Run horses of the night
Run at breakneck speed
Hurry burn your hooves
Shed sparks be lightning
Keep me from dying in this darkness
Bring the sun out
Bring the sun out
(Father sun in your heat and light
Bring life breath)
Rid the moon of its fake light
(scraps of your generous light)
Shed it on ocean on tree on child
Burn the forests blue.

From The Daughter of Jesus

We ended up in Corsica
A small place lapped by waters all around
And we'd grown tired by then
He struggled with my name
Seraph was his first instinct
Settled (gloriously) for Luce
He loved light
After those long hours in the dark tomb

"They never really shut the rock wheel
tightly enough. Mary snuck me out."

He smiled a tight smile
(His frozen face muscles would
Not allow for more)

He knew what came ahead
("A joyful curse" he said):
Thoreau, Dr King
While revering the Buddha

He wept when he thought of honest
Monks and nuns lost to love

"Things are clear
I can see angels on trees
Names"

Yes yes she was my mother
And she was no whore
She glowed like Venus in her quiet ways
Kneaded His flesh
Smoothed His tight eyebrows
She healed Him
Softened his skin with unguents
Opened His eyes with her eyes
(The look of ocean
                      and Winds
            Birds wings)

She chewed hard food
Grains
And fed Him by hand
Like a bird
Fed him water from her drenched hair

EQUALITY

And that's always been Her story –
Banned for biting the apple,
For wanting to know

Branded dirty, impure for giving birth

Only vestal virgins go to heaven, not the mother of Jesus

Boys hunt them down like wingless she-birds
Then blame them for being caught in nets

Let the blood flow on dusty floors

(and let death follow)

EARLY FALL EAST BRUNSWICH'S POND
BY THE PUBLIC LIBRARY
(for Steven Barnhart)

The world of God metes out its sweet boredom
Not one tree is untouched by Fall
Bunches of leaves surrounded by brown halo
Small squirrels sniff and scratch soaked woodchips
The aerator shoots out
Three climbing waterfalls
So carp can keep on living
Geese work their wide wings
Croak and run across the pond
Signs for Peace, scarves,
Embrace a young birch
Next to a marble monument
For boys and girls lost to the last war

Inside the library
Sleek fans
Drones pinned to the ceiling
Scatter cool air

Measured click clock of heels
Of old women ambling
To the latte counter

Fast flip flop of children
Rushing to computers
An aged man forming poetry
On two pink scraps of paper

SONG
> "But the foreigners stayed on…"

There is always a great woman
who will sing for us,
who will keen,
when we are born,
(restart the world),
when we are dead.
Remembering orange orchards,
she will sing of roots,
of seeds,
of rainstorms,
of earth, swellings,
of air, burning,
of rain, bending, hoarding.
She will sing of seed exploding
into wings,
of light splashing
in earth's innards,
of flames swirling,
solar winds.

The Dead Speak

Grandfather says, "Scrub

my tombstone. Give me flowers,

white flowers, chrysanthemums.

Cut the grass.

Don't stay too long."

HEAVEN

Last day of June. Slim,
lazy gods, deer doe and
fawns,
a family of four,
cross the northwest corner
of my house. Clouds re--
lease
the sun. Trees let through
a modest breeze. My wine
jug
is half full. Am I in heaven?

HAWKS AT PRE-DAWN IN NEW JERSEY

Nine hawks dance
over the northern Parkway
strip
just off exit 105.
Lit by the two crooked
candles of the waning half
moon
and the sun mounting over
the ocean,
they glide, soft as owls,
certain as top ten ice
dancers
cavorting on a rink in Man-
asquan.

To a would-be Iago

Old barracuda face, you,
whose crawling hate
has shaped your jaws
into anvils of steel,
you, whose teeth stick out
like the horns of the moon,
why me?
Is it my bountiful lover?
My children's beauty?
Is it my poetry
that keeps you
endlessly roaming
like a requiem shark,
forever and forever puking
bits of coagulated blood?
O man, whose ugliness
sends children howling
under their mothers' skirts,
are hate and envy
your only slop?

Ragusa, Sicily

Always the children rushing like small sparrows,
Their little bruises needing care
From older sisters or grandmothers.
Play never stopped with their quick tears –
Bread munched in the breakaway at tag,
A hurried drink at the public fountain before hide and seek,
Or while players were being chosen for a soccer game.
And always the church bells like comforting songs –
Night and day, night and day,
Louder and sharper for the holidays,
Or on the day of the dead when widows,
Rosaries wrapped around their wrists like chains,
Wailed like witches.

A Cannon Fired a Shot
(for Paul Francisco)

As my father swung his rig
through one lane roads
and over wooden bridges,
I grew dumb.
The Pennsylania sky
was cinnamon rum.
A cannon fired a shot.
We slowly came to a halt
as my father's voice
brightened me. "Son."
In the fields ahead,
a two-horse cart swam in hay.
The driver, his white shirt
like a flower, held the reins.
Then lightning cracked
and the cart rose drowning in red.
Freed, the horses whinnied and ran.
The man lay dead, burning in the hay.
My father murmured,
"All we know
is that He has saved us
for another day."

Chimney Birds
(for M.G.)

Ten birds in the year
will fly down the chimney
(the echo of beating wings,
cries of lost children
within that hollowness).
Something pulls them in –
the smell of fire in stone,
the suck of wind.
Down through the throat they fall
and fly about the house.
None takes the open window out.
To let them go,
I catch them in my hands,
and hold them like warm hearts.

A Woman Runs Out of the Mental Health Clinic

You veer to your right,
into the traffic,
holding your baby in our arms,
screaming at "bastards and
bitches." Your husband
tries to match your swift steps
and nudges you to your left,
where the car waits
like a tomb on wheels.
He orders you into
decorum. "Eleanor…
stop it…enough."
Your screams reach a higher
pitch. "How dare she?
The bitch…the bitch."
You weep, and baby,
close to your heart
and used to your confusion
and rage, does not wake.

An End

No sandpiper has visited.
Summer rolls down the hill,
a stone loosened by rain and dampness
and the hiss of time.
This early Saturday in August,
and sun comes up at two-thirty
and the ocean stinks
dragging brown puke on its back.
The seagulls do no sing,
silent at the edge of water.
A rust and silver pigeon
moves heavy-footed.
Drowned feathers, burned wood
smash against rocks.
(And you elsewhere.)

Ancestral Chimera

I lay stored in Ionian loins,
deliniated in the green lines of warriors' chins.
Farmers' bins fed me.
The lip of the scythe freely smacked wheat stalks,
the flowered grain plenty as rain.
My thighs held horse flanks,
my hands combed mane.
Lightning singed the skies for me.
Birds beat the Morse codes of Gods with their cries.
And I made chartered wreaths with my words,
set wailing shrouds.
In chilling nights, I sang for the runaway moon,
and she listened.
I danced for the sun my father,
danced in the longer days –
watered jasmine buds with my sweat,
and the white-leaved flower followed.

To a Schizophrenic

Your brain will not sift chaff from grain,
rake pale weed into garbage heaps
and hoard the good sunblood.
To you, each bit, gold or crap,
lights up the universal black.

Faith

Soldiers with limbs like frost,
lost boys,
climb up from those shallow ditches,
swim up from the mile-long sea.
Father, Father,
Save up from
A Fall
Father, Father,
Let Mother
Bless us all
Soldiers with limbs like frost,
lost boys,
do not slouch, mechanical,
but pirouette to wild waltzes –
dance to the stars,
spin to the northern lights
Father, Father,
Save us from
A Fall
Father, Father,
Let Mother
Bless us all
Soldiers with limbs like frost,
lost boys,

hose clean the slaughterhouse
of a Beelzebub named Hitler –
same the dream of fields of poppies
charred by early frost,
joy at the low skies,
bounce babies in your arms
and catch them like falling birds
Father, Father
Save us from
A Fall
Father, Father,
Let Mother
Bless us all

Only

Only the ones with wings fall:
The fliers to the sun
(oh, Icarus, my son)
The storm riders
The rainbow skaters
The ugly who sense beauty in their song
The children who reinvent the world
(oh Lord, oh Lord)

From the Mountain

I

Emily Dickinson walked deeply into it
Water like snakes swirling up her thighs, the sea
Sea gulls screech over it
Dive into it, rest on it
Fly over it standing still
Hold the wind under their wings, the sea –
Descend, descend, and find
The dunes, wheat fields churning bread
In the wind
The coo-coo birds singing the advent of
Spring.

II

The divining rod
Will lead you to water
You can drink
(is dead Beatrice's hair
in the winds, or did
Dante fake the whole thing?)
Go past the dune

And find the ocean in the wind
You will
And when you're hungry
Walk along the river
Lift a rock here and there
And find small crabs
For supper
Under burning sticks
Hunger the wick

III

See the dance
Of the rainbow's wanderings
When the sun spins west
And shoots over breaking waves
There there in the rainbow
Is the spirit
In the cracking spume

IV

Where is the reason in the snow?
Sugar and lemon
Make it ice cream –
A clean mix
Miracle of physics
And chemistry?
Water flowing at 33?

V

Where is the harm?

VI

The gathering of wheat
At summer's end, presaging
The fall
Riding on a small donkey
To the farm
Stumping on wheat stalks
Scattering them to the sky
On late afternoons
Watching the chaff
Being eaten by the winds
The leftovers settling
On peach trees
Then the gathering of fallen grain
The trek to the wind mill
Flower and then bread

VII

Dark matter
Dark matter
Let me open your innards
Let's look into your womb
'a veder
La luce che sfolgora'
Just as there is

Light inside the hardest
Darkest seed
Just as there is light
Just as the cosmos is
 Light and heat
Just as it congregates
Coagulates –
Each planet is a drop of blood
Each living sun
Energy churning
Attracting pulling
Small matter
Drawing it
Into a solar tribe
Bivouacs
Interspersed
And giving a center to the
Universe.

Where Are the Tamers of Horses?

Where are the tamers of horses?
Are they all dead?
Did they all quit after Hector's
Death-mound was raised?
Was he the last rider of wild horses?
Or are our worst still the only ones
Full of passionate intensity
Did Yeats call it right?
Justice sepulchred by penny gatherers
And power brokers:

>	A Marilyn Monroe cardinal in New York
>	 The cindered Castro brothers hugging the pope
>	 Soup kitchens in the homeland!

The Dead Rise

The dead rise recycled
galactic-eyed infants
Open wide
Rich in silences
Seeing watching
Waiting for the warm breasts of a mother
For the strong shoulders of a father
The dead come back
Bringing song
Bringing solar winds
Moon phases
The breath of ocean winds
Garbage heaps flowers
Dirt blossoms
The holiness of petals and filth

Kryseis

Generous in all ways
Your sapphire eyes
Spin like the late afternoon's midway waves
On the eastern sea
As the early setting sun swirls
Rainbows into their spins –
Deep as longing
Deep as the pull of kiss
Or the joining of birds
And nest –
Open like an endless eddy your mind
The golden root of a black hole
That siphons into symphony –
Your tongue
Your hands make fire of my body

What is the Wind?

The wind's an unfurled flag today,
undulating, whipping like a snake, nipping…

The wind's a tomboy today, ponytail tucked under a pink cap,
practicing football punts on bunches of dry leaves…

The wind's a nun in white habit today, swirling
with hot breath the loose surface of deep snow…

The wind's a fiend today, snickering friend,
hellbent for freedom, remembering mountain tops,
Grand Canyon dips, OCEAN, OCEAN, OCEAN…

Genesis

A woman sails into the burgeoning wave
And wails: "Keep off the drowning hordes,
The earth-rotted algae. The red sail
Will turn into shroud, and the shore
Will be littered with children and porpoises."
The earth instructs:
"Be steady, look for her in the mud.
She is there, as usual,
But this time she will be a stranger.
Dig in the mud and slime."

Stay the Course

Once you set out to sea stay the course
Head for the open waters
Even if the wind shouts the sails into shreads
Even if the mast is swallowed by flying serpents
Stay the course
Even if the sand bars and rocks strip the ship's body
Stay the course
Head for open waters – the blue
At all costs stay away from the land

I Sing
(for D.T.)

I sing lovers
Lost in the heat of sweat
Mindless loose
The energy of unwinding
Muscle and gristle
Cooling blood
I sing the oval eye of child
Ready to tear
To laugh at sun or rain
I sing the newborn
Unfolding
The mystery of the first
Breath
Dirt ocean
The drive to crawl

Schizoid Carousel

a tree standing tall
is parallel when seen from a side glance
and sailing south enough
will turn the earth on its head
with nor left or right
or front or back
or up or down
we ride a schizoid carousel
where cheap chrome is
silver
and butterfly wing
is gold
god speaks to us
from the large eyes of children
set deep in their small heads
those eyes
what lakes
those eyes

In the Manner of W. Shakespeare
(in a modern way)

"I am myself alone"
because "I am what I am"
open-winged
light-lifted yet
aware of my ingenuity
and careless charm
one who will commit an instant's sin
not calculated like the false grin
of some
we live on this dirt speck
a pimple in the constellation of sun
crawling in the blood and mud
of unfulfilled yearnings and
corked desires
cursing those who move
among clear waters,
themselves their own lakes.

The Immortality of Nothingness

whatever fire you will spark
will out
sooner or later
the sun or grandmother's brazier
ask Beethoven or Bach
wood will eat itself
as will the tongue of wind
as will the song of child

About the Author

EMANUEL DI PASQUALE was born in Ragusa, Sicily, and emigrated to America in 1957. He earned a Master of Arts from New York University in 1966. Since then, he has taught college English. His translations from the Italian include *Sharing a Trip* by Silvio Ramat (2000); *Infinite Present* (co-translated with Michael Palma, 2001); *The Journey Ends Here* by Carlo della Corte; *Between the Blast Furnaces and the Dizzyness* by Milo De Angelis; and Dante's *Vita nuova* (2011). His poetry books in English include *Genesis* (1989); *The Silver Lake Love Poems* (2000); *Escapes the Night* (2001); *Carthweel to the Moon* (2003); *Writing Anew: New and Selected Poems* (2007); *Siciliana* (2009); and *Harvest Sun* (2011). Sections of his poetry book *Genesis* were translated into Italian by Carmela Muscarà (with an introduction by Giovanni Occhipinti) with the title *Un'ambra prigioniera* (2002). He lives in front of the Atlantic Ocean with his daughter, Elisabeth Raffaela.

AWARDS: Bordighera Poetry Prize for translating Joe Salerno's *Song of the Tulip Tree* into Italian (1998); Academy of American Poets' Raiziss/de Palchi Fellowship for translating Silvio Ramat's *Sharing a Trip* into English (2000); Chelsea Poetry Award for *Connections: Prose Poems of Rome, Sicily, and Venice* (2002); National Italian American Foundation grant for translating contemporary Italian poets into English (2002).

VIA FOLIOS
A refereed book series dedicated to the culture of Italians and Italian Americans.

CAROSONE & LOGIUDICE. *Our Naked Lives*. Vol 87 Essays. $15
JAMES PERICONI, *Strangers in a Strange Land*, Vol. 86. Literary Criticism, $24
DANIELA GIOSEFFI, *Escaping La Vita Della Cucina*, Vol. 85. Essays & Creative Writing. $22
MARIA FAMÀ, *Mystics in the Family*, Vol. 84. Poetry, $10
ROSSANA DEL ZIO, *From Bread and Tomatoes to Zuppa di Pesce "Ciambotto"*, Vol. 83. $15
LORENZO DELBOCA, *Polentoni*, Vol. 82. Italian Studies, $15
SAMUEL GHELLI, *A Reference Grammar*, Vol. 81. Italian Language. $36
ROSS TALARICO, *Sled Run*, Vol. 80. Fiction. $15
FRED MISURELLA, *Only Sons*, Vol. 79. Fiction. $14
FRANK LENTRICCHIA, *The Portable Lentricchia*, Vol. 78. Fiction. $16
RICHARD VETERE, *The Other Colors in a Snow Storm*, Vol. 77. Poetry. $10
GARIBALDI LAPOLLA, *Fire in the Flesh*, Vol. 76 Fiction & Criticism. $25
GEORGE GUIDA, *The Pope Stories*, Vol. 75 Prose. $15
ROBERT VISCUSI, *Ellis Island*, Vol. 74. Poetry. $28
ELENA GIANINI BELOTTI, *The Bitter Taste of Strangers Bread*, Vol. 73, Fiction, $24
PINO APRILE, *Terroni*, Vol. 72, Italian Studies, $20
EMANUEL DI PASQUALE, *Harvest*, Vol. 71, Poetry, $10
ROBERT ZWEIG, *Return to Naples*, Vol. 70, Memoir, $16
AIROS & CAPPELLI, *Guido*, Vol. 69, Italian/American Studies, $12
FRED GARDAPHÉ, *Moustache Pete is Dead! Long Live Moustache Pete!*, Vol. 67, Literature/Oral History, $12
PAOLO RUFFILLI, *Dark Room/Camera oscura*, Vol. 66, Poetry, $11
HELEN BAROLINI, *Crossing the Alps*, Vol. 65, Fiction, $14
COSMO FERRARA, *Profiles of Italian Americans*, Vol. 64, Italian Americana, $16
GIL FAGIANI, *Chianti in Connecticut*, Vol. 63, Poetry, $10
BASSETTI & D'ACQUINO, *Italic Lessons*, Vol. 62, Italian/American Studies, $10
CAVALIERI & PASCARELLI, Eds., *The Poet's Cookbook*, Vol. 61, Poetry/Recipes, $12
EMANUEL DI PASQUALE, *Siciliana*, Vol. 60, Poetry, $8
NATALIA COSTA, Ed., *Bufalini*, Vol. 59, Poetry. $18.
RICHARD VETERE, *Baroque*, Vol. 58, Fiction. $18.
LEWIS TURCO, *La Famiglia/The Family*, Vol. 57, Memoir, $15
NICK JAMES MILETI, *The Unscrupulous*, Vol. 56, Humanities, $20
BASSETTI, ACCOLLA, D'AQUINO, *Italici: An Encounter with Piero Bassetti*, Vol. 55, Italian Studies, $8
GIOSE RIMANELLI, *The Three-legged One*, Vol. 54, Fiction, $15
CHARLES KLOPP, *Bele Antiche Stòrie*, Vol. 53, Criticism, $25
JOSEPH RICAPITO, *Second Wave*, Vol. 52, Poetry, $12
GARY MORMINO, *Italians in Florida*, Vol. 51, History, $15
GIANFRANCO ANGELUCCI, *Federico F.*, Vol. 50, Fiction, $15
ANTHONY VALERIO, *The Little Sailor*, Vol. 49, Memoir, $9
ROSS TALARICO, *The Reptilian Interludes*, Vol. 48, Poetry, $15
RACHEL GUIDO DE VRIES, *Teeny Tiny Tino's Fishing Story*, Vol. 47, Children's Literature, $6
EMANUEL DI PASQUALE, *Writing Anew*, Vol. 46, Poetry, $15
MARIA FAMÀ, *Looking For Cover*, Vol. 45, Poetry, $12
ANTHONY VALERIO, *Toni Cade Bambara's One Sicilian Night*, Vol. 44, Poetry, $10
EMANUEL CARNEVALI, Dennis Barone, Ed., *Furnished Rooms*, Vol. 43, Poetry, $14
BRENT ADKINS, et al., Ed., *Shifting Borders, Negotiating Places*, Vol. 42, Proceedings, $18

GEORGE GUIDA, *Low Italian*, Vol. 41, Poetry, $11
GARDAPHÈ, GIORDANO, TAMBURRI, *Introducing Italian Americana*, Vol. 40, Italian/American Studies, $10
DANIELA GIOSEFFI, *Blood Autumn/Autunno di sangue*, Vol. 39, Poetry, $15/$25
FRED MISURELLA, *Lies to Live by*, Vol. 38, Stories, $15
STEVEN BELLUSCIO, *Constructing a Bibliography*, Vol. 37, Italian Americana, $15
ANTHONY JULIAN TAMBURRI, Ed., *Italian Cultural Studies 2002*, Vol. 36, Essays, $18
BEA TUSIANI, *con amore*, Vol. 35, Memoir, $19
FLAVIA BRIZIO-SKOV, Ed., *Reconstructing Societies in the Aftermath of War*, Vol. 34, History, $30
TAMBURRI, et al., Eds., *Italian Cultural Studies 2001*, Vol. 33, Essays, $18
ELIZABETH G. MESSINA, Ed., *In Our Own Voices*, Vol. 32, Italian/American Studies, $25
STANISLAO G. PUGLIESE, *Desperate Inscriptions*, Vol. 31, History, $12
HOSTERT & TAMBURRI, Eds., *Screening Ethnicity*, Vol. 30, Italian/American Culture, $25
G. PARATI & B. LAWTON, Eds., *Italian Cultural Studies*, Vol. 29, Essays, $18
HELEN BAROLINI, *More Italian Hours*, Vol. 28, Fiction, $16
FRANCO NASI, Ed., *Intorno alla Via Emilia*, Vol. 27, Culture, $16
ARTHUR L. CLEMENTS, *The Book of Madness & Love*, Vol. 26, Poetry, $10
JOHN CASEY, et al., *Imagining Humanity*, Vol. 25, Interdisciplinary Studies, $18
ROBERT LIMA, *Sardinia/Sardegna*, Vol. 24, Poetry, $10
DANIELA GIOSEFFI, *Going On*, Vol. 23, Poetry, $10
ROSS TALARICO, *The Journey Home*, Vol. 22, Poetry, $12
EMANUEL DI PASQUALE, *The Silver Lake Love Poems*, Vol. 21, Poetry, $7
JOSEPH TUSIANI, *Ethnicity*, Vol. 20, Poetry, $12
JENNIFER LAGIER, *Second Class Citizen*, Vol. 19, Poetry, $8
FELIX STEFANILE, *The Country of Absence*, Vol. 18, Poetry, $9
PHILIP CANNISTRARO, *Blackshirts*, Vol. 17, History, $12
LUIGI RUSTICHELLI, Ed., *Seminario sul racconto*, Vol. 16, Narrative, $10
LEWIS TURCO, *Shaking the Family Tree*, Vol. 15, Memoirs, $9
LUIGI RUSTICHELLI, Ed., *Seminario sulla drammaturgia*, Vol. 14, Theater/Essays, $10
FRED GARDAPHÈ, *Moustache Pete is Dead! Long Live Moustache Pete!*, Vol. 13, Oral Literature, $10
JONE GAILLARD CORSI, *Il libretto d'autore*, 1860–1930, Vol. 12, Criticism, $17
HELEN BAROLINI, *Chiaroscuro: Essays of Identity*, Vol. 11, Essays, $15
PICARAZZI & FEINSTEIN, Eds., *An African Harlequin in Milan*, Vol. 10, Theater/Essays, $15
JOSEPH RICAPITO, *Florentine Streets & Other Poems*, Vol. 9, Poetry, $9
FRED MISURELLA, *Short Time*, Vol. 8, Novella, $7
NED CONDINI, *Quartettsatz*, Vol. 7, Poetry, $7
ANTHONY JULIAN TAMBURRI, Ed., *Fuori: Essays by Italian/American Lesbians and Gays*, Vol. 6, Essays, $10
ANTONIO GRAMSCI, P. Verdicchio, Trans. & Intro., *The Southern Question*, Vol. 5, Social Criticism, $5
DANIELA GIOSEFFI, *Word Wounds & Water Flowers*, Vol. 4, Poetry, $8
WILEY FEINSTEIN, *Humility's Deceit: Calvino Reading Ariosto Reading Calvino*, Vol. 3, Criticism, $10
PAOLO A. GIORDANO, Ed., *Joseph Tusiani: Poet, Translator, Humanist*, Vol. 2, Criticism, $25
ROBERT VISCUSI, *Oration Upon the Most Recent Death of Christopher Columbus*, Vol. 1, Poetry, $3

Published by Bordighera, Inc., an independently owned not-for-profit scholarly organization that has no legal affiliation to the University of Florida or to the John D. Calandra Italian American Institute, Queens College, The City University of New York.